THE
SILENT CITY

EREZ YAKIN

WITH AN INTRODUCTION BY YEVGENY YEVTUSHENKO

KITCHEN SINK PRESS

NORTHAMPTON, MASSACHUSETTS

AG
YAK

Library of Congress Cataloging-in-Publication Data

Yakin, Erez.
    The silent city / by Erez Yakin ; introduction by Yevgeny
Yevtushenko.
        p.   cm.
    ISBN 0-87816-385-9 (pbk.)
    I. Yevtushenko, Yevgeny Aleksandrovich, 1933-   . II. Title.
PN6727.Y35S57 1995
741.5'973--dc20   95-39748
                                                         CIP

First Printing: October 1995

5 4 3 2 1

For a free catalog of comics, books, and related merchandise,
write to the above Kitchen Sink Press address, or call 1-800-365-SINK (7465).

ACKNOWLEDGEMENTS

My thanks to my parents, Mina and Moni, and to my brother Boaz. A special thank you to Ira Gallen, whose care and efforts made this publication possible. I also want to thank Denis Kitchen for believing in my work, Yevgeny Yevtushenko and Albert Todd for their generous contributions, Phil Amara, Amie Brockway and Brendan Stephens for their insight and input, and Carlos Melendez, Laura Salinger, Naomi Nakao and Muriel Broadman for their support.

THE SCREAM OF SILENCE

Art is not altogether helpless before the face of history. It not only reflects it, but transforms it. Without diminishing the role of art to mere obstinate pedagogy, one right cannot be taken away from it—the right to warn humanity against danger.

Silent City is a scream of danger for you and your children. Possibly it is the beginning of a new breed of visual novel. It is not the visual version of another novel, nor a collection of carefully selected illustrations; it is a self-sufficient, independent work, not written by a writer, but envisioned by an artist. Although it is enigmatic, there is a story that glows like grape seeds through the skin of the grape. It leaves room for conjecture, but its unwritten text will resound in the heart of anyone who reads it. This novel warns us of a potential "gulagocaust," and it is extraordinary that this warning was produced when the author was only seventeen years old.

When I was teaching at the University of Tulsa, I received a letter from a retired professor who maintained that the Holocaust never happened. He argued that the prison bars were not real, but only figments of imagination. In Russia there are also people who maintain that the "Archipelago of Gulags" described by Solzhenitsyn never happened. It is therefore especially important that Yakin, by virtue of his age, never having been in either Hitler's or Stalin's concentration camps, is able to believe in them, not simply as the reality of the past, but as a mortally dangerous variant of the future.

Fortunately for us all, George Orwell was mistaken in his hypnotic sketch of a totalitarian society in his novel *1984*. But perhaps, thanks precisely to such writers as Jack London (*The Iron Heel*), Yevgeny Zamyatin (*We*), and Orwell himself, who horrified us with their ominous visions of the future, they did not become reality. (We have not even yet fully appreciated the role of Charlie Chaplin's film *The Great Dictator* in the destruction of Nazism and its moral discreditation.) Dostoyevski's novel *The Possessed* was a scream of danger that was not heard by his contemporaries. Because they didn't hear it, calling the novel reactionary, the scream was transformed into the scream of the tortured during Stalin's terror.

Erez Yakin was born when there was still the last gasp of terror of that monster totalitarian empire that called itself the socialist camp. With socialism it had no relationship, but with a camp the relationship was direct. When Yakin was born, refugees trying to make their way across the Berlin Wall were still being shot, dissidents were still being sentenced to psychiatric detention, Sakharov was still in Gorky, Solzhenitsyn was still in exile, and *Doctor Zhivago* was still not published in its homeland.

That empire has now collapsed. But was Ronald Reagan right, having called the Soviet Union alone the "Evil Empire"? If that were so, then with the end of that empire all mankind would have found itself in paradise. But that didn't happen—and could not happen—because the "Evil Empire" is within each of us. We look about us and we see repulsive splashes of fascism—now in Germany, now in England, now even in Russia, where twenty-six million lives were lost in the war against fascism. Even half-Jewish Zhirinovsky makes anti-Semitism a card that brings him support of twenty-three percent of the voters.

Without a doubt Erez Yakin is not acquainted with the Russian painter Oleg Tselkov, now living in Paris. Once, about the year of Yakin's birth, this artist in the Soviet Union had an exhibition with an all-time record for brevity. It was closed by KGB agents in an hour. Why? Because they were terrified by Tselkov's characters on canvas similar to Yakin's—robot-like creatures that have lost all individuality, either because they are executioners, victims, or simply deformed foliage in the automobile cemetery of history. But is this the vision of the future?

In spite of all the talk about democracy and the rights of man, individuality inexorably gets washed away. Bureaucracy, whether state or corporate, very easily becomes a kind of fascism and the faces of major leaders, overflowing with feelings of their own imaginary greatness, are very much like the faces of the S.S. of the future in the canvases of Tselkov or the drawings of Yakin.

In Yakin's silent city, how heart-rending is the tiny window in a prison wall, where perhaps there once were other tiny windows that are now bricked up, and the lonely silhouette visible through the bars. But who bricked up the other windows and probably will soon brick up this last one? The prisoners themselves; involuntary victims of totalitarianism, the masons of their own prisons.

At another window, a character disfigured by thoughts unexpressed has turned away in despair from the unbearable industrial landscape. Is this Socrates of totalitarianism doomed to silence? Slaves with hammers on their shoulders are mere appendages to the landscape. Are they still able to understand that they are slaves? I once wrote:

Only free man
thinks he is a slave.

Erez Yakin screams with the silence of his drawings. His power lies in his fear of becoming a slave whose exhausted face, bleached pale by work in gloomy, sunless dungeons, is caressed only by drying rags on a laundry line, fluttering seagulls of farewell from the past. I have seen such rags, left hanging for many years on the terraces of abandoned Greek homes on the Turkish side of Cyprus, hardened to stone from the ocean's salt.

God grant that we ourselves do not become fossilized rags. We want to be alive and not turned to stone. It is that human right that we must never permit any dictatorship to *take* from us—not the dictatorship of police, nor the dictatorship of chaos, nor the dictatorship of money. And as long as there are youths like Erez Yakin, I believe that everything turned to stone will nevertheless be conquered by the living. I believe that those of the prison world will not succeed in walling up all the windows, just as they have not walled up the eyes of this beautifully talented artist who gives us warning so that we will not walk on that damned road where there is the smell of ashes of those who once were alive.

— YEVGENY YEVTUSHENKO
May 1994

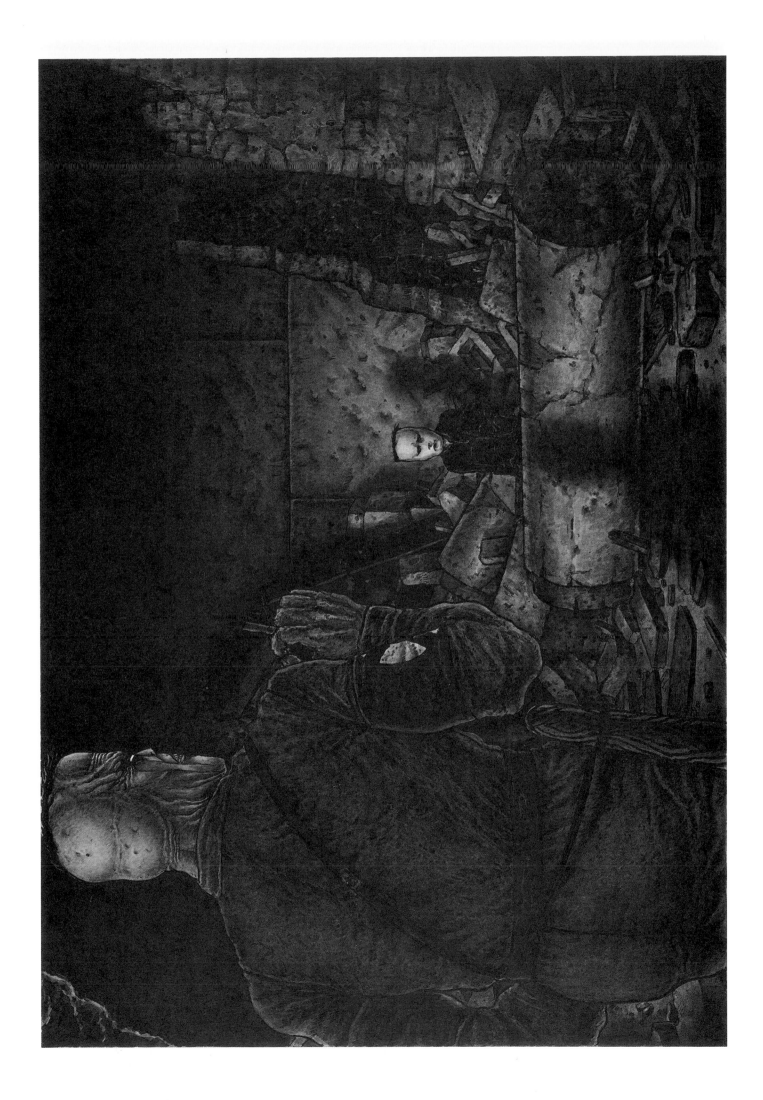

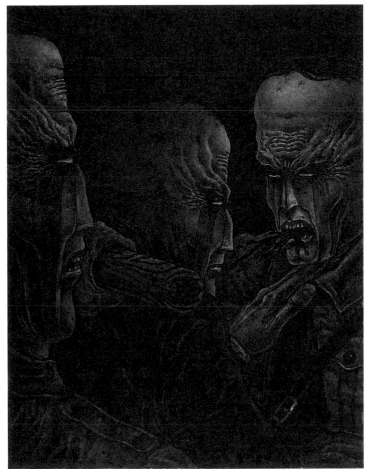

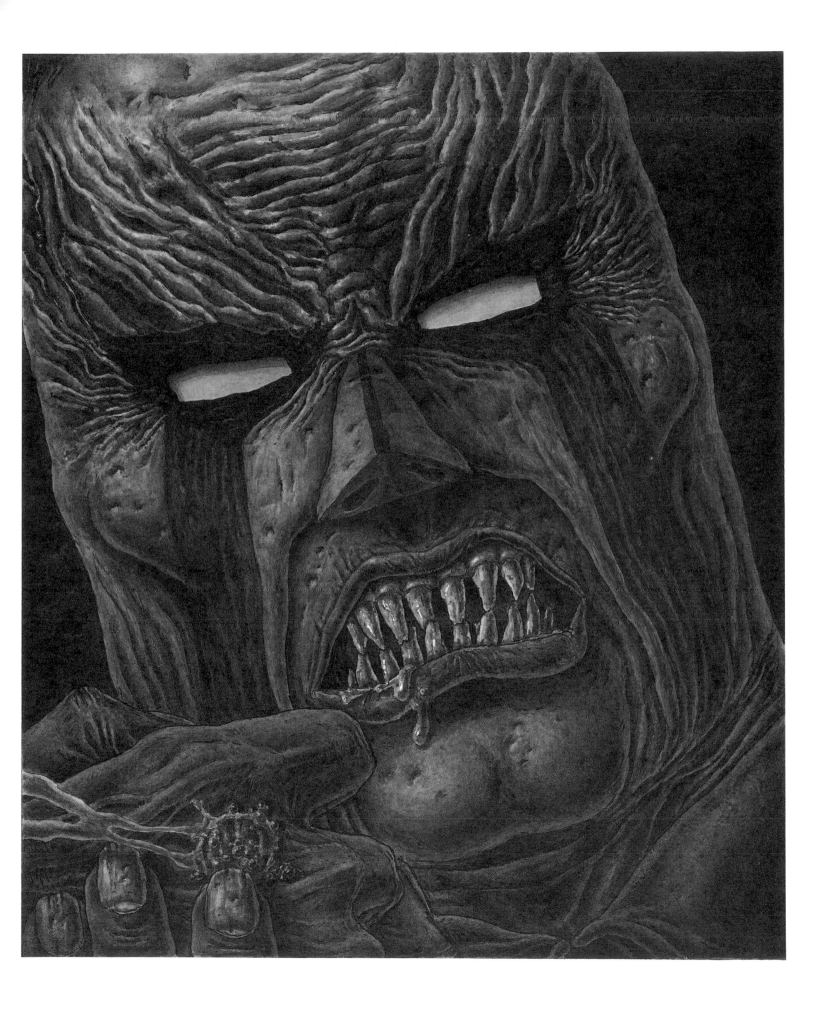

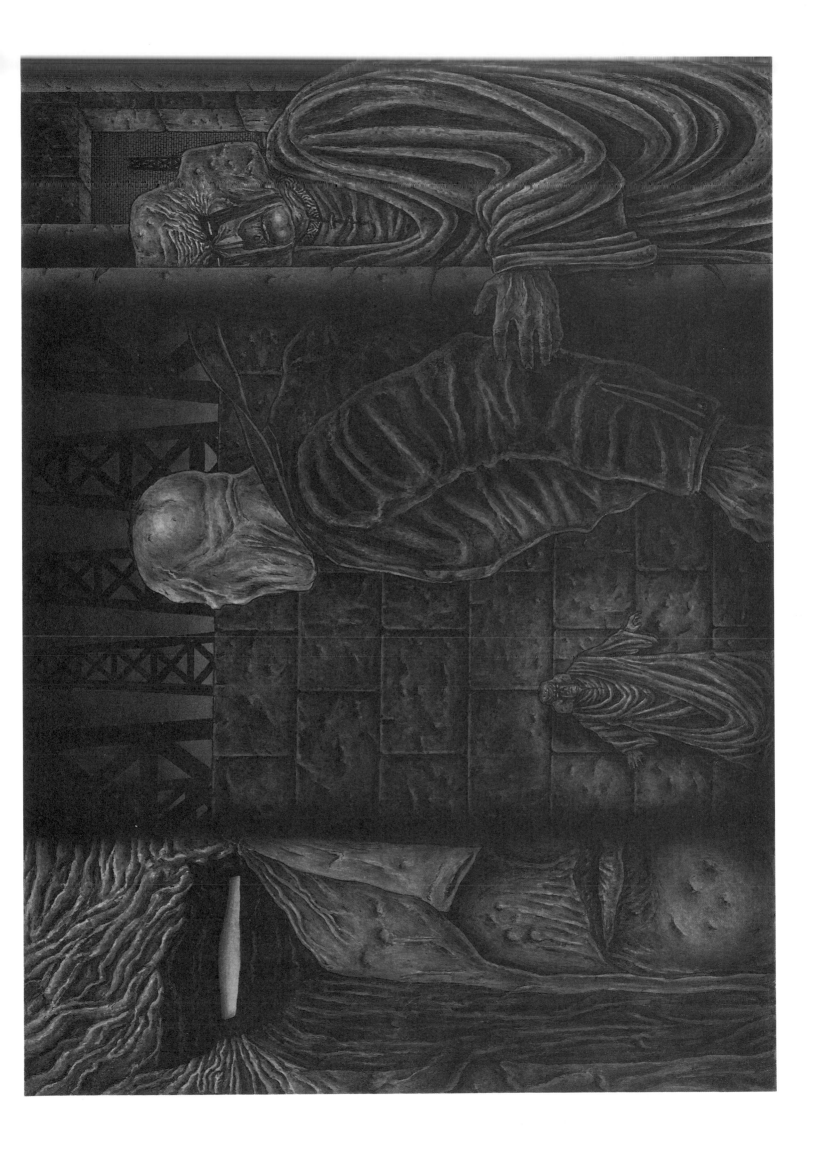

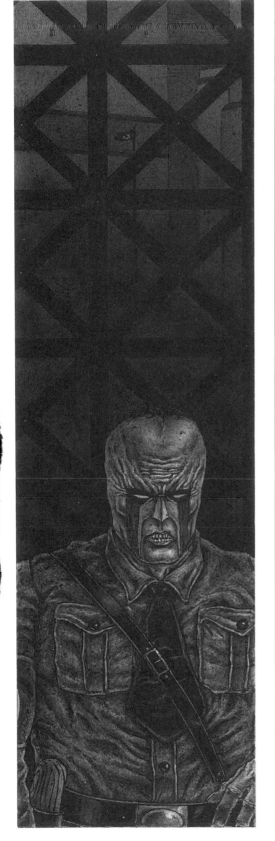

EREZ YAKIN *completed* The Silent City *in 1988 at the age of eighteen. His current works include a forthcoming novel entitled* The River, *which is also silent, and a series of prints entitled* Dark Hours. *He was born in New York City, where he lives and works today.*

YEVGENY YEVTUSHENKO *is known worldwide as a poet, writer, filmmaker and political voice. His works include* The Collected Poems, 1952-1990, Fatal Half-Measures, *and the screenplay to Mikhail Kalatozov's* I Am Cuba. *He currently lives in Russia.*